WATERSPORTS GUIDE TO

Cancun

Isla Mujeres, Playa del Carmen, Akumal, and Tulum

Susanne and Stuart Cummings

Pisces Books™
A division of Gulf Publishing Company
Houston, Texas

Publisher's note: At the time of publication of this book, all the information was determined to be as accurate as possible. However, when you use this guide, new construction may have changed land reference points, weather may have altered reef configurations, and some businesses may no longer be in operation. Your assistance in keeping future editions up-to-date will be greatly appreciated.

Also, please pay particular attention to the diver rating system in this book. Know your limits!

Pisces Books
A division of Gulf Publishing Company
P.O. Box 2608, Houston, Texas 77252-2608

Library of Congress Cataloging-in-Publication Data

Cummings, Stuart.
Watersports guide to Cancun/Stuart and Susanne Cummings.
p. cm.
Includes index.
ISBN 1-55992-073-4
1. Skin diving—Mexico—Cancun—Guidebooks. 2. Scuba diving—Mexico—Cancun—Guidebooks. 3. Cancun (Mexico)—Guidebooks. I. Cummings, Susanne. II. Title.
GV840.S78C85 1993
797.2'3—dc20 93-15534
CIP

Printed in Hong Kong

10 9 8 7 6 5 4 3 2 1

Table of Contents

Acknowledgments

We would like to express our appreciation to the following companies and individuals whose extreme generosity with their time, assistance, and cooperation was invaluable to the preparation of this guide:

Caribbean Sports
Continental Villas Plaza, Cancun
Continental Plaza Playacar, Playa del Carmen
Dacor Corporation
Denizen Wetsuits
Henderson Wetsuits
Iberia Airlines
Las Palapas, Playa del Carmen
Marina Aqua Ray, Cancun
Mexican Tourism Marketing, Inc.
Oceanic USA
Playacar Divers, Playa del Carmen
Progressive Public Relations, Inc.
SeaPro

The white-spot filefish is not very common, but a sharp eye may detect one or two on Keep Reef.

Yellow trumpetfish can often be found hiding among the soft corals.

How to Use This Guide

This guide is designed to acquaint you with a variety of the best and most popular dive sites in Cancun and Playa del Carmen and to provide useful information that will help you decide whether a particular location is appropriate for your abilities and intended dive plan, e.g. macro vs. wide angle photography, drift dive, wall dive vs. shallow reef dive, etc. The dive sites described in this guide represent only a sampling of the sites in each area.

In Chapters 5 and 6, you will find a dive-site-by-dive-site description of the special features of individual sites and information regarding recommended skill levels. The experience levels are repeated in a condensed format at the beginning of these chapters.

Cancun's current swept reefs explode with vibrant color.

Thousands of divers come to enjoy the clear Caribbean waters of the Yucatan each year.

Regardless of how you choose to use this guide—either reading it from cover to cover or selecting sections of interest—certain chapters should be viewed as required reading. Chapter 7 on "Smart, Safe Diving" is of primary importance. No matter how much we think we know or remember, we can always benefit from a refresher. The section on "Reef Etiquette and Buoyancy Control" in Chapter 7 focuses on how to help preserve our fragile marine environment and be ecologically responsible divers. We hope the tips in this section will help you make a personal contribution to preserving our delicate reef system and make you a more skillful diver. If you plan to keep diving into your senior years, wouldn't it be nice to have something beautiful to look at?

Although this guide is directed at people who enjoy spending a substantial amount of time in or under the water, everyone has to come up for air. And because some surface intervals are longer than others, we have provided a brief overview in Chapter 1 of the history, geography, accommodations, and activities of Cancun and the Cancun-Tulum Corridor. If you have been to this unique part of Mexico, you obviously enjoyed your stay enough to consider returning. But don't imagine that just because you've seen one part of the Mexican Caribbean, you've seen it all. Each resort area offers its own unique ambiance, its own distinctive personality. If you have never experienced any of them, get ready for some wonderful discoveries and surprises.

The Rating System for Divers and Dives

Our suggestions as to the minimum level of expertise required for any given dive should be taken in a conservative sense, keeping in mind the old adage about there being old divers and bold divers, but few old bold divers.

We have rated the dive sites based on the following qualifications: A *novice* diver is in decent physical condition and has recently completed a basic open water certification diving course by an internationally recognized certifying agency, or is a certified diver who has not been diving recently (within the last 12 months), or is a certified diver who has no experience in similar waters. An *intermediate* diver is a certified diver in excellent physical condition, has been diving actively for at least a year following a basic open water course, and has been diving recently (within the last 6 months) in similar waters. An *advanced* diver has completed an advanced certification diving course, has been diving recently in similar waters, and is in excellent physical condition.

Cancun's fabulous Hotel Zone sits on a 14-mile-long sandbar.

A diver enjoys one of the many coral encrusted caves in the Cancun area.

If you are not sure which category you fit, ask the advice of a local divemaster or instructor. You will find a list at the end of this guide of all the dive and watersports operators along the Cancun-Tulum Corridor. They are best qualified to assess your abilities based on the prevailing dive conditions at any given site. Be honest about your qualifications—diving "over your head" can be an unpleasant and uncomfortable experience. If you're still in doubt, ask a divemaster or instructor to accompany you on the first dive in new waters.

If you haven't been diving for 12 months or more, you and your equipment may need a checkout. Make sure your equipment, especially your regulator, is in top condition. If your skills are a little rusty or you are using new and unfamiliar equipment for the first time, take a refresher dive in the pool with your local dive store at home or when you arrive in Mexico with an instructor at a dive center.

Resort Courses

If you've never been scuba diving but always wanted to, most of the dive operators in Cancun and along the Cancun-Tulum Corridor offer "resort courses," which allow you to "discover" scuba diving to see if it's your cup of tea before you invest a lot of time and money in a full certification course.

The resort course entails a half-day orientation, which includes some basic theory, practice with equipment and tanks in a pool or shallow water, and a one-tank dive to 12 to 30 feet in the ocean at a safe dive site accompanied by your instructor.

If you find you like the sensation of exploring the marine world close up and personal, you'll find scuba diving addictive!

A resort course is a popular way to try diving in an easy and affordable way.

1

Overview of Cancun and the Mexican Caribbean

The beautiful coastline of the Mexican Caribbean lies on the eastern edge of the state of Quintana Roo on the Yucatan Peninsula. It is a region bordered by glimmering white sand beaches and aquamarine waters on one side, and on the other side it is dominated by dense verdant jungle that conceals the mysteries of the ancient Mayan civilization. Until a dozen or so years ago, this tropical paradise was accessible to the few who had the time, money, and adventurous spirit to enjoy its natural and unspoiled treasures. Today, Cancun is a world-class resort and even the quieter, more secluded towns along the coast to the south are being targeted for tourism development. But despite the transformation, the Mexican Caribbean retains its charm and allure for all who make the pilgrimage.

Even the most dedicated sunbathers can't resist a dip in Cancun's warm ocean waters.

History

To understand the mystique of the Mexican Caribbean, you must first explore its beginnings in a highly developed and sophisticated Mayan civilization. In the 10th century, their vast cities and ceremonial centers were in an irreversible decline, their widespread influence diminishing rapidly. By the 16th century, when the Spanish arrived, little of the grandeur of the once vast civilization remained.

Isolated from the rest of Mexico by jungles, lagoons, and swamps, the jungle eventually overran and concealed the ruins of these extraordinary cities. It was only until the latter part of this century that some of the thousands of Mayan sites covering over 2,400 square kilometers of land have been accessible to archaeologists and tourists.

Geography and Climate

Along the Caribbean coastline of Quintana Roo, long stretches of aquamarine waters, diamond white beaches, and lush green vegetation are occa-

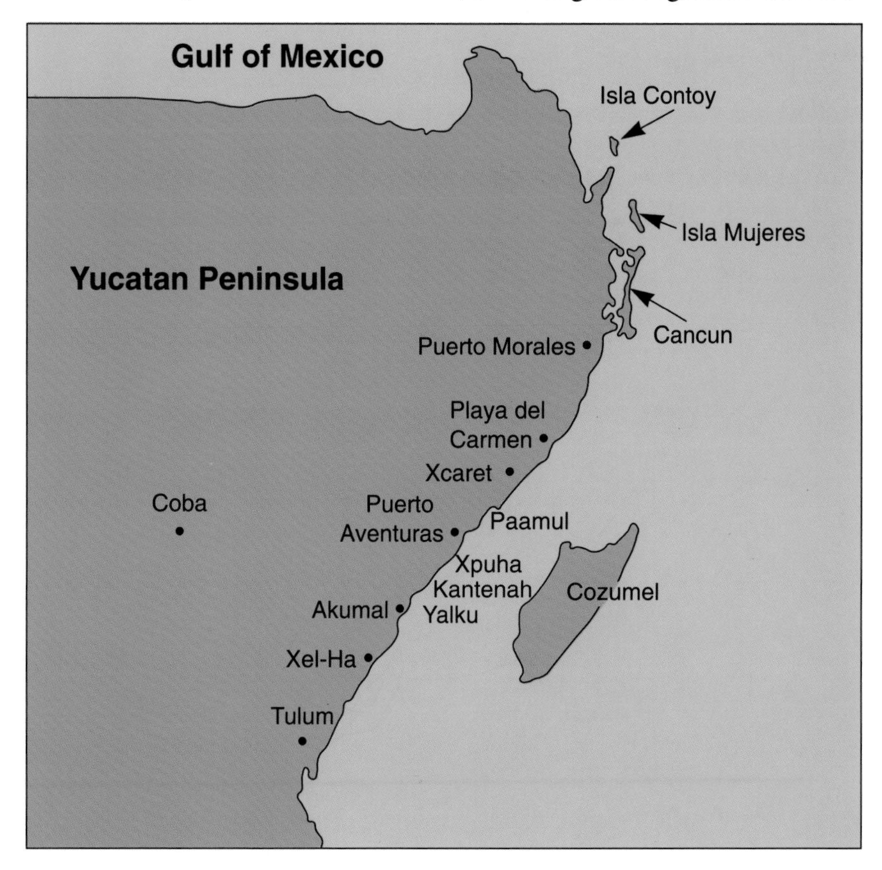

sionally broken by jagged rocky outcroppings, coves, and inlets. Inland from the shore, an emerald expanse of jungle hides secret lagoons and cenotes.

The Mexican Caribbean is known for its superb weather, with 200 sunny, rainless days a year, less annual rainfall than in the Virgin Islands or the Bahamas, and temperatures averaging around 80°F with a variance of around 5° either way.

The summer months are hot and dry. Even though the Yucatan is not in the hurricane belt, hurricane season can bring some rainy, gusty weather to the area. The rainy season is in the late fall and winter and you may even see some rain at the beginning of June and September. During the winter season, the evenings can get a little cool, so pack a light sweater. In general, dress is informal, but in Cancun some restaurants are more elegant.

Local Services and Information

Currency: Mexican pesos are the local currency, but everyone will accept American dollars. No coins, please! If you use U.S. currency, expect to receive your change in pesos.

Time Zone: Mexico is in the Central Time Zone. They do not observe Daylight Savings Time.

Postal Service: Air mail letters or postcards to the U.S. or Canada cost about 60 cents per 20 grams (or about 85 cents per ounce). If you're in a hurry, Federal Express service is available.

Tourists from every corner of the globe flock to Cancun's miles of cool, white beaches.

Telephone Service: Local payphones accept 100-peso coins for local or collect calls. In Cancun, many hotels offer "dial direct" AT&T service for long distance calls to the U.S. and Canada. If you're calling collect or operator assisted from your hotel, expect a hefty service charge.

Credit Cards: Major hotels, resorts, restaurants and stores, especially in Cancun, accept all major credit cards such as MasterCard, VISA, and American Express. Smaller establishments, especially once you leave the modernity of Cancun, may require cash or travelers' checks.

Car Rental: Renting a car in Mexico is a little different from in the U.S. Before you sign a contract, check the car over carefully, make sure it has a good spare tire and tools, and that at least some of your tires have visible treads. Take insurance because most likely your U.S. insurance won't cover anything that happens in Mexico. Beyond Cancun, gas stations are rare so make sure you start out with a full tank of gas. Car rentals are expensive, but in Mexico feel free to bargain. If you are not planning on using a car extensively, you might consider traveling by taxi. They are relatively inexpensive and can be hired by the hour or the day for excursions.

Electricity: 110 volt AC.

Transportation: Cancun is only an hour-and-twenty-minute flight from Miami, and direct service is available from several major U.S. gateway cities on several airlines. The newest airline to offer service is Iberia Airlines. Cancun's International Airport is located only 11 miles from the Hotel Zone. If your final destination is any other point along the Mexican Caribbean, it is necessary to fly into Cancun and continue your travel from there. (You can also fly into Cozumel and take the ferry to Playa del Carmen.)

Tourists can enjoy excellent service on Iberia Airlines, the newest airline to offer regularly scheduled service to Cancun International Airport from Miami.

Customs and Immigration: Proof of citizenship and a tourist card are required for entry into Mexico. Tourist cards are provided free of charge at any Mexican embassy, consulate, tourist office, airline ticket counter, or travel agency serving Mexico for US and Canadian citizens. Keep a copy of your tourist card with you for departure from Mexico.

Cancun—Activities and Accommodations

Centuries ago, Mayan kings vacationed in Cancun amid pyramids and temples. Today, modern-day sun worshippers bask in the pleasures of a truly contemporary resort. The beaches are among Mexico's most beautiful. The clear, vivid turquoise waters are tantalizing. The sun shines almost all year round.

Cancun is a planned resort built by the Mexican government's FONATUR (National Fund for Tourism Promotion and Development) as its first multimillion-dollar experiment in resort development. It opened in 1974 with only two hotels in the Hotel Zone. Today, it is a thriving resort with facilities that surpass international standards. By 1995, Cancun anticipates a total capacity of over 20,000 hotel rooms and 2.8 million visitors a year. Currently, Cancun entertains more tourists each year than Bermuda, Jamaica, and the Virgin Islands.

It is truly a mega-resort with everything from great beaches and watersports to nightlife and shopping. Whatever your pleasure, you'll find it in Cancun.

Beaches: Cancun is essentially a 14 mile-long sandbar connected by two bridges, one at each end to Cancun City and the mainland. In other words, it's one long powdery white beach! Composed of old limestone, the sand always feels cool and comfortable, even under the hottest tropical sun.

The Continental Villas Plaza is one of Cancun's luxurious five-star resorts.

Isla Contoy

If you find yourself in need of a break from the hustle and bustle of Cancun, two hours by boat from either Cancun or Isla Mujeres is Isla Contoy, the only uninhabited island in the Mexican Caribbean. A coral island where more than 70 species of birds are in permanent residence, Isla Contoy is a national wildlife reserve and bird sanctuary. It is common to see sea gulls, pelicans, frigates, petrels, cormorants, heron and a variety of other sea birds during your visit. At some times of the year, you may glimpse the more exotic rose-colored spoonbills, long-necked egrets and brown boobies. The photography opportunities are almost endless.

Declared a national preserve in 1961 by the Mexican government, this small island remains pristine and undeveloped with the exception of a small museum. There visitors can learn about the island's geology, hydrology, climate, fauna and aviary life. It is tranquil, uncrowded and natural.

It is also a place for the environmentally aware. Littering is forbidden and you are not permitted to remove anything from the island. No overnight stays are allowed, but bring your snorkeling gear with you because you'll have ample opportunity to explore the unspoiled reefs that surround the island. At the northern end of Isla Contoy, the reefs lie in 15 to 20 feet of water. Just off the beach on the eastern side of the island, you can pay an underwater visit to the sunken vessel, Las Calderas.

Each year, Isla Contoy becomes the focus of attention for the annual lobster run when hordes of the tasty crustaceans meet at the island's northernmost point in anticipation of the strong northerly wind that will transport them across the shallows.

Daily ferry service to Isla Contoy is available from Cancun and Isla Mujeres.

Almost all of the hotels in Cancun's Hotel Zone have their own beaches. There are also several beautiful public beaches that provide changing facilities, restaurants, and bars for the convenience of visitors.

The beaches located on Bahia de Mujeres, where the water is calm and protected, are excellent for swimming. Swimming, however, is *not* recommended at the beaches facing the Caribbean because undertows and strong currents can make it particularly hazardous.

Watersports: (See Chapter 3)

Shoppers visiting Cancun will be delighted by the modern malls that carry local and international goods.

Accommodations: You'll find no shortage of hotel rooms in Cancun. There is an abundance of large and more intimate full-service resorts on the island. Several offer excellent value packages with airfare from major gateways in the U.S. throughout the year. For the economy minded, less expensive accommodations can be found at hotels in Cancun City. Good and affordable bus service between the city and the Hotel Zone makes transportation to the beaches and restaurants in the Hotel Zone easily accessible.

Shopping: Cancun is a freeport, which means it is a virtual paradise for those who know a good buy when they see one. Modern upscale U.S.-style malls and native markets offer everything from local crafts like jewelry, handwoven clothing, and popular Yucatan hammocks to the finest American and European-made products. Handicrafts and contemporary resort wear are the best buys as well as sterling silver jewelry with semi-precious stones. The

Some of the best buys in the Mexican Caribbean are the handcrafted local merchandise.

Local artisans often demonstrate their work on the sidewalks.

Ki-Huic open market is filled with traditional Mexican crafts from all over the country. Many shops close between 2 and 4 pm for the traditional afternoon siesta, but most stay open in the evening for the tourists.

Dining and Nightlife: Few Mexican resorts offer such a wide variety of restaurants, more than 300 of them in the Hotel Zone and downtown. You'll find sophisticated French cuisine in a French provincial setting with old-world charm, action-packed places that have live music at night, ultra-romantic tables-for-two, hideaways overlooking the lagoon or in a downtown garden setting, Mexican food and entertainment in a colonial style courtyard or local gathering places where everyone eats and meets . . . sooner or later. Menus feature everything from fresh seafood dishes, traditional Mexican specialties, French and Italian cuisine to Chinese and Polynesian delights. Mouth-watering traditional Yucatan food such as chicken or suckling pig baked in banana leaves, venison or the famous "sopa de lima" should definitely be sampled. Only the daring should try the extremely hot "habanera" chili which grows nowhere else in Mexico!

Entertainment: Those who love nightlife will be swept away by the glittering assortment of clubs and dazzling discos in Cancun. Performances of the Folkloric Ballet take place almost every night. Mexican Fiesta Nights

There are more than 300 restaurants in Cancun including many of international reputation.

are staged around twice each week. You can see a Polynesian show in the Mauna Loa Shopping Center, flamenco dancers from Spain, or sail away on the Tropical Cruiser for an unforgettable "Pirate's Night" adventure. You can even see a bullfight in the true Mexican tradition on Wednesday afternoons. There are fiestas and cultural events year-round and guests are welcome to participate in the celebrations.

Sightseeing: A vacation in Cancun is not complete without a trip to one of the many places of interest surrounding Cancun. A wide variety of day-trips are offered by numerous local tour operators. Island excursions to Isla Mujeres, Isla Contoy, or Cozumel enable visitors to experience a different side of Mexican lifestyle. History buffs can explore the ancient Mayan ruins of Chichen Itza or Tulum. Bus and boat tours are offered year-round and reservations can be arranged by your hotel. If you are traveling from point to point in Cancun, taxis are abundant. There is also convenient bus service, or you can rent a car, scooter, or bicycle. If you plan on the latter, beware. The roads are narrow, curvy, and the locals drive very fast!

Spanish flamenco dancers entertain guests at one of Cancun's popular night spots.

Playa del Carmen is well-known for its beautiful, uncrowded beaches.

Isla Mujeres may be quaint and laid-back, but shoppers will find plenty of fine stores in which to browse.

Isla Mujeres

A few miles off Cancun's shores lies Isla Mujeres, a laid-back paradise for snorkelers, divers, and barefoot beachcombers alike. Only five miles long and half a mile wide, the island is well known for its exquisite beaches, beautiful reefs, and quaint town dotted by colorful old fishing boats and waterfront cantinas.

The island's history dates back to the Mayans, when it was a pilgrimage site. In 1517, it was discovered by the Spanish who named it "isle of women" for the stone figures of Ix-chel, the Mayan goddess of fertility, which they found scattered around the island on their arrival.

In the 17th, 18th, and 19th centuries, it was a haven for pirates. The ruins of Hacienda Mundaca, once the home of the Spanish pirate and slave trader Fermin Mundaca, can still be seen. According to legend, this notorious pirate decided to turn over a new leaf. He promptly burned his ship, murdered his crew, and fell in love with a local woman. He built the stately hacienda to woo her, but, alas, she had other plans and ran away with her lover. Mundaca followed her to Merida and there he died of unrequited love. There is an empty tomb on the island in his memory.

Despite the island's rather colorful history, its beaches and quaint charm are what attract visitors. The passenger ferries from Cancun run hourly to the main and only town on the island. Its narrow streets are lined with excellent local shops, and waterfront restaurants offer an authentic Mexican ambiance and good food. Although there is a lovely beach within walking distance from downtown, a visit to El Garrafon beach is a must.

Just off the beach is an underwater national park where divers and snorkelers can explore a shallow coral reef inhabited by an extensive variety of vividly colored tropical fish. There are old anchors and cannons from a sunken Spanish vessel. You may even see some turtles here. In 1990, some 60,000 baby turtles were released in the surrounding waters as part of a turtle protection program on the island. You can rent diving and snorkeling gear at El Garrafon if you prefer not to bring your own. It is ideally suited to snorkeling and beginner divers. But plan to arrive early, especially during high tourist season. The popular beach and underwater park can get crowded.

Isla Mujeres is one of the most popular day-trips for visitors to Cancun.

The Cancun-Tulum Corridor—Including Playa del Carmen and Akumal

Cancun is by no means for those looking for quiet and privacy. But travel southward along the Mexican Caribbean to what has become known as the Cancun-Tulum Corridor, and you'll discover 100 miles of unspoiled beaches, uninhabited except for a few small fishing villages and some recently developed resorts.

The intimate ambiance of Las Palapas resort attracts an international clientele.

With the opening of the first-class Continental Plaza Playacar, Playa del Carmen had its first full-service luxury resort.

Yet even with what seems to be a growing trend toward large resort developments along this stretch of coastline, you can still find quiet beaches with no footprints but your own, secluded coves, and quaint Mexican ambiance in the charming fishing villages that dot the road. Regardless of whether you choose to stay in five-star hotels and resorts or any of the local campgrounds, you'll still find plenty of secluded beaches and shady palm trees to call your own during your stay.

The coastline is dotted with small towns that appeal to the more adventurous tourist for their off-the-beaten track atmosphere. At any one of them, you'll be able to savor a taste of the real Mexico.

If you can live without all the amenities of a big resort, the small slow-paced fishing village of **Puerto Morales** is worth a stopover. You won't find extensive accommodations here, but they are inexpensive and camping is allowed. When you order seafood, you'll be served the catch of the day, often prepared right on the beach at one of the local beachfront restaurants.

Alternatively, **Playa del Carmen** offers all the amenities of a large resort without forfeiting its rustic, charming character. You'll find a variety of accommodations ranging from full-service resorts, small hotels, and villas to private homes for rent.

In Mayan times, Playa del Carmen was called Haman Ha. Pilgrims crossing the channel to Cozumel, which was a sacred island, departed from here. Today, Playa del Carmen is still primarily known by tourists as a departure point for the local ferries that travel back and forth between Cozumel and the mainland. It is also a popular port-of-call for cruise ships that

Continental Plaza Playacar is situated on one of the most beautiful stretches of beach in Playa del Carmen.

anchor just offshore in the early morning hours to drop off passengers on day-tours to Tulum and Xel-ha. It is an excellent starting point for anyone planning to explore the many fascinating points of interest along the coast. Unfortunately, it isn't always easy to pull yourself away from the little local cafes or the casual beach parties.

There are several small mini-malls and more traditional Mexican shops, so the shopping is certainly sufficient to satisfy discriminating shoppers. Additionally, although neighboring Cancun and Cozumel may have more shopping and a wider variety of stores, the somewhat lower prices in Playa del Carmen should be attractive to bargain hunters.

There is no shortage of restaurants in Playa del Carmen either, especially for those who like the relaxed ambiance of open-air restaurants on the beach. The quantity and quality will ensure that you don't get tired or bored and, most likely, you'll discover a few that you want to return to again and again.

Most activity is centered around the ferry pier and the town center where ferry passengers come and go all day and into the evening. The ferry ride to Cozumel takes about 40 to 60 minutes, depending on which ferry you take. The price runs anywhere from $2.00US to $5.00US. The ferry is scheduled to depart every half hour and, for the most part, it runs on time.

Despite the increased traffic and development that Playa del Carmen is experiencing, it retains much of its quaintness and charm.

The Cancun-Tulum Corridor offers numerous excellent snorkeling sites right off the beaches.

Although not known for its shopping, Playa del Carmen has many fine shops and some of the best prices in the Mexican Caribbean.

As you travel southward from Playa del Carmen, you'll find the new 500-acre resort community of **Puerto Aventuras,** which primarily caters to sailing and yachting enthusiasts with a full-service 240-slip marina that is equipped to take care of even the most luxurious of yachts. Puerto Aventuras also has a CEDAM nautical museum, a five-star PADI dive center, dolphin encounter experience, and windsurfing facilities.

Every year from late spring through the summer, sea turtles visit the beaches of **Akumal** to lay their eggs, hence its name, which means "land of the turtles" in Mayan. Year-round, tourists seek the understated charm of this small fishing village. For better or worse, Akumal has recently been discovered by the resort developers and now has several hotel and condo developments with more to come. But there are still small hotels, villas, and guest houses as well, and, so far, the palm-tree lined beaches, clear waters, and lush surrounding jungle remain intact. If you are staying in Akumal, include Xel-Ha on your list of day-trips.

Yucatan's Underwater Caves

At first glance, you may think the Yucatan Peninsula is a solid mass of landfall. In fact, a vast labyrinth of underwater caves lies below the surface.

Two hundred and fifty million years ago, the Yucatan Peninsula was covered by the sea. As geological time passed, the level of the ocean varied, ultimately leaving the peninsula partially or completely dry. The soft, porous limestone composition of the peninsula, however, made it susceptible to erosion caused by the tropical rainfall. Gradually, the fresh water permeated the surface and sculpted increasingly larger openings below.

When water levels dropped even farther during the Ice Age, the dripping rain water left calcium carbonate deposits, which over thousands and thousands of years produced dramatic stalactites, stalagmites, columns, and flow stones. Eventually, as we all know, the Ice Age ended, the ice receded and the water levels increased substantially. The caves were flooded and preserved under water for the last ten thousand years.

This intricate system of underwater caves is a recent discovery, and most of it remains unexplored. But some parts of the system are accessible and divers with the proper specialized training and experience can participate in this adventure of a lifetime.

2

Archaeological Sites

In Mexico, archaeology is an integral part of everyday life. All along the coast of the Mexican Caribbean, ruins of ancient Mayan settlements can be found. In Cancun itself, Mayan ruins are scattered throughout the Hotel Zone. But the most extraordinary remnants of the great Mayan civilization can be found at Chichen Itza, Tulum and Coba.

Tulum is the only Mayan ruins located on the ocean. ▶

The Yucatan is known for its Mayan ruins, and Xcaret is no exception.

Tips to Maximize Enjoyment of Your Vacation

- Bring comfortable footwear if you plan to explore the architectural sites. Climbing a pyramid in sandals can be hazardous.
- Bring a good sunscreen and use it. The tropical sun is strong even in the winter months and a vacation is no time to nurse a sunburn.
- Don't drink the water. Avoid consuming the local water at all costs and that means ice cubes and frozen drinks made with ice cubes! Use bottled water only, which you can purchase at local stores. While the margaritas may look tempting on a hot day, you're better off with a bottle of excellent Mexican beer or a soft drink. Try your beer Mexican style—with a wedge of lime!

Chichen Itza

Undoubtedly the most famous of all late Mayan cities, Chichen Itza has been a holy place to the Mayans for centuries. Its imposing pyramids, temples, plumed serpents carved in stone, and a sacrificial well recall their ancient world. Its structures date back to around A.D. 450 and weathered the widespread collapse of the Mayans 400 years later. About 100 years later, it was revived under the Toltecs and flourished for another 200 years until it was finally abandoned in about 1224. When the Spaniards arrived in the 1500s, Chichen Itza was once again overrun by jungle.

The various buildings at Chichen Itza cover a six-square-mile area. Many of them reflect the differences in the earlier pure Mayan and later Toltec-influenced architecture. The most famous is the Temple of Kukulkan, the god of fertility, which rests atop a 75-foot-high pyramid. Here the pyramid dramatically demonstrates the special genius of Mayan astronomers and architects. Twice a year, at the spring and fall equinox, the afternoon sun creates a shadow effect on the upper temple steps of the pyramid of the serpent god Kukulkan and descends the 91 steps to earth to fertilize and replenish it. In the evenings, sound and light shows are presented.

Chichen Itza is located 125 miles west of Cancun. You can drive it in about 2.5 hours or enjoy one of the many excursions offered by Cancun's tour operators. Chichen Itza also has a small airport with flights from Cancun, and tour packages are available that include accommodations near the ruins.

◀ *You never know where you'll meet a new friend when you're visiting the friendly Mexican Caribbean.*

Tulum

Seventy-eight miles south of Cancun lie the ancient ruins of Tulum, once a thriving Mayan seaport and spiritual center. Today, more than 60 temples and structures, which probably date back to the 13th century Mayan-Toltec period, have been excavated at this site. The most prominent building is a dramatic pyramid situated at the edge of the cliff overlooking the beach. The climb up the steep stone steps requires nothing less than an act of bravery!

While its architecture may not be as elaborate as that of Chichen Itza, it makes up for it with a spectacular view of the Caribbean from its cliff-side perch. It appears to be the only Mayan city located on the ocean and the only walled Mayan city in existence. It is thought that, while other great Mayan cities had been abandoned, Tulum was still inhabited in 1518 when the Spanish conquerors arrived on its shores. What had the Mayans felt when they first spotted Spanish ships approaching their small, seaside city?

One of the most photogenic sites along the Mexican Caribbean, Tulum is an ideal excursion from just about anywhere from Cancun southward. It is about a 90-minute drive from Cancun and several tour operators run day-trips to Tulum daily.

Coba

Heading inland from Tulum about 30 miles through the rainforest are the ruins of Coba, a classic settlement that reached its pinnacle around A.D. 500 to 800. It was once a heavily populated trade center where 16 ceremonial highways made of limestone converged. It was never discovered by the Spanish. It was, however, discovered by archaeologists in 1972. It is the largest Mayan city that has been uncovered to date and most of it remains unexcavated. At 120 feet high, the Nohuch-Mul pyramid towers over the jungle that surrounds Coba and gives visitors a superb view of the unexcavated mounds around it.

Not only a haven for archaeology enthusiasts, Coba is a treat for bird lovers with more than 200 species visiting its nearby lagoon and jungle lakes each year. Coba's unspoiled state has become an attractive lure to visitors.

If you visit Coba, be sure to bring a sufficient supply of insect repellent with you. The bugs in this jungle location can be abundant and aggressive, especially in the early morning or late afternoon hours.

The outdoor market at Tulum is an ideal place to purchase local arts and crafts as well as inexpensive souvenirs. ▶

CANCUN

Watersports

Unlike many diving and snorkeling destinations in the Caribbean, the resorts along the Cancun-Tulum Corridor and, in particular, Cancun, offer much more in the way of watersports activities. Let your imagination run wild! The beachfront resort that doesn't offer a plethora of watersports options is rare. With miles of sparkling white sand beaches, you can enjoy the sun and surf to your heart's content and in the style of your personal choosing.

Conditions are excellent for windsurfing, water-skiing and jet-skiing. Windsurfing has become one of world's most popular resort sports. All you need is a sailboard, a lot of water, and just the right amount of constant wind. Cancun has the right ingredients in the right amounts to make it one of the best windsurfing destinations in the Caribbean. Several of Cancun's mari-

Marina Aqua Ray's 40-foot snorkel boat takes guests on a tour of the mangroves on the way to a shallow reef.

Taking a ride in a parasail is one of the best ways to get a bird's eye view of Cancun.

nas specialize in the sport. Board rentals and instruction are available at several hotels and with about two to three hours of instruction, you should be moving upright and under sail power. And although you may not be ready to participate in the National Windsurfing Tournament that is held in Can-

Sailing is a fun and economical way to enjoy the Mexican Caribbean.

The Jungle Tour combines the fun of wave runners, snorkeling, and a tour of the mangroves all in one affordable excursion.

cun annually, you can still "cop some air" along the shore of Bahia de Mujeres or in Laguna Nichupte.

In Cancun, the calm glassy surface of Nichupte Lagoon is the perfect place to water-ski whether you're a novice just learning or a veteran of the sport. Local marinas have professional water-skiers on staff who can offer instruction, helpful tips, and safety guidelines.

The constant Caribbean trade winds make windsurfing one of the most popular sports along the Mexican Caribbean.

Most visitors find a half-hour rental on a wave runner is plenty of time to enjoy the freedom of this "water motorcycle."

Jet-skiing seems to be the latest rage. It takes almost no time to learn the finer points of the art of doing wheelies on your jet ski or wave runner. These one-person motor scooters can reach speeds of up to 35 mph and they stop if you fall off, so you can't lose them. Local marinas will rent you equipment and provide instruction if you've never been on one before. Remember—it may not be difficult to master but it takes a surprising amount of energy and stamina. For most of us, a half-hour rental is more than enough the first time out!

If you're vacationing in Cancun, you can combine the fun of riding a two-person wave runner with a fascinating excursion into the mangroves that surround the lagoon on a half-day "jungle boat tour." Bring your snorkel gear, because the itinerary includes ample time to cool off in the clear, tropical waters and take a first-hand look at the activity below!

Boat lovers can indulge in just about every kind of water toy imaginable. You can sail away in Hobie cat or sunfish, paddle to paradise in a canoe or kayak, float to nowhere in an inflatable raft or inner tube, or cover a lot of territory in little time in a power boat. Boats can be chartered with or without crew and, in Cancun, you can hitch a ride on a mini-sub or glass-bottom boat which lets you see what's underwater without getting wet.

Parasailing also attracts its loyal following of adventurers. If you've never soared in one, you've missed the experience of a vacation. State of

Marina Aqua Ray's two Australian-built semi-submersibles are great ways to enjoy the coral reefs around Cancun without getting wet.

the art technology means you're just about guaranteed not to get wet on take-off or landing.

There are few sensations that can equal the rush of feeling a fighting fish firmly grab the end of your line. Sportfishing means big action with white marlin, bluefin tuna, and sailfish running in the summer and grouper, snapper, mackerel, bonito, wahoo, barracuda, and tuna ready to challenge your skill and determination year-round. In addition to deep-sea fishing, you can fish in the lagoon. Bonefishing is also a popular pastime. Experienced and knowledgeable guides are available to take you to the best spots and most charters include gear, bait, beer, and crew.

Passengers photograph and videotape the reefs in the cool, dry comfort of air-conditioned semi-submersibles.

For the underwater adventurers, don your snorkel or dive gear and take the plunge into the rich and prolific waters of the Mexican Caribbean. You're likely to be surprised by what you'll encounter.

Puerto Aventuras

Puerto Aventuras is like its own "shangri-la" in the jungle with hotels, villas, night life, shopping, a dive shop, and a "swim with the dolphins" program that is not to be missed. Unlike the highly publicized dolphin encounter program at Xcaret, where sometimes as many as a dozen or more humans are permitted in the water at the same time with three to five dolphins, Puerto Aventuras "Dolphin Discovery" program limits the number of people who visit with the dolphins during any single encounter. The result is a far less crowded and more intimate experience in which both dolphins and swimmers seem to enjoy the interaction thoroughly.

The swim program lasts about an hour. It begins with a 15-minute educational video about dolphins and a 15-minute instruction session with the dolphin trainer. The last 30 minutes are enjoyed in the water with the dolphins.

If you want to document your swim, "Dolphin Discovery" will shoot a personalized video of you and the dolphins at play for an additional charge. You can watch the video immediately after your swim and it's a very professionally done video complete with slow motion action shots and music.

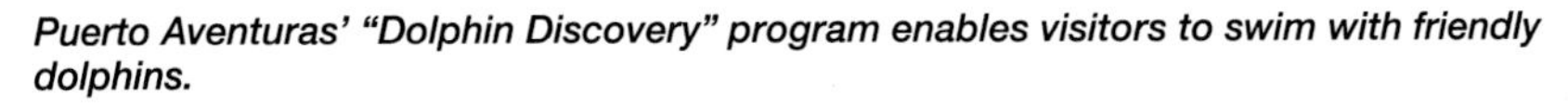

Puerto Aventuras' "Dolphin Discovery" program enables visitors to swim with friendly dolphins.

4

Diving and Snorkeling Along the Cancun-Tulum Corridor

It's no wonder that diving and snorkeling are so popular in Caribbean waters of Yucatan peninsula. White sand beaches blend gently into the aquamarine waters that veil the second largest barrier reef in the world. Underwater reefs, canyons, walls, and caves that display 65 species of corals, as well as colorful sponges and algae, provide a natural habitat for a thriving community of marine creatures, large and small.

Diving conditions along the Cancun-Tulum Corridor can vary significantly with the seasons and prevailing weather conditions. Although visibility underwater can sometimes reach 100 feet or more, generally, it averages 50–70 feet, sometimes better and only occasionally worse.

There is almost always some current at the dive sites along the Mexican Caribbean coast. The current varies depending on the time of year and the prevailing weather conditions and tends to be stronger at sites that are unprotected from the open ocean. Often, if the current is somewhat strong, divemasters will do a drift dive, enabling divers to float along the reef with the current and be picked up by the boat at the point at which they surface. If the current is strong at the surface but diminished at the reef, divemasters may put down a descent/ascent line to enable divers to reach the bottom without struggling and consuming air unnecessarily.

Most of the dive operators in Cancun and along the coast transport divers to the reefs in small "fast boats." They are not luxuriously outfitted, but they do the job efficiently. More often than not, they do not have biminis or any shade from the hot tropical sun, so be sure to bring a hat or visor, a t-shirt, and sunblock.

Playa del Carmen's reefs are inhabited by a wide variety of marine creatures typical of the Mexican Caribbean. ►

Ferries start running between Cozumel and Playa del Carmen as early as 5:30 a.m.

When you're snorkeling along the reefs, it's a good idea to take along a snorkeling buddy.

The beaches along the Cancun-Tulum Corridor tend to be less populated than those in Cancun.

Diving and snorkeling in Cancun and Playa del Carmen are discussed in greater detail in the following chapters. But there are a lot of opportunities and places to submerge along the Cancun-Tulum Corridor that are well worth the plunge.

Beginning at Puerto Morelos, you'll find good reefs offshore with good visibility. Although it's a small and untouristy fishing town, snorkeling and diving trips can be easily arranged.

Puerto Aventuras is a newly developed tourist destination where the focus is on water-oriented activities. Divers will find a full service five-star P.A.D.I. dive facility, a CEDAM nautical museum displaying relics from sunken ships, and a good selection of offshore dive sites to explore.

The quiet beach resort of Akumal is tucked away on a palm-lined bay bordered by brushland about 65 miles south of Cancun. The headquarters of

Even though Playa del Carmen faces to the east, the sunsets can be spectacular.

Carved out of the jungle, Puerto Aventuras offers accommodations, dining, and watersports facilities.

the Mexican Underwater Explorers Club, divers are familiar with Akumal's fine snorkeling and scuba. The bay is protected by a barrier reef that runs parallel to the shore where divers will find canyons and long tunnels, shallow reefs, hard and soft coral growth, as well as an abundance of tropical fish life.

There is also an "underwater museum" offshore where divers can investigate the remnants and sunken "treasures" of old coral encrusted anchors and guns of the *Matanceros,* a Spanish galleon shipwrecked in 1741.

Akumal is an ideal "find" for avid divers who want great diving without the crowds of the more popular and publicized Caribbean destinations. Sites such as La Tortuga, which is frequented by large turtles that gave Akumal its name, the Nets with its canyons and tunnels, and Aquarium, where nurse sharks can often be found beneath archlike formations, all make diving in Akumal exciting. In particular, the unique caves and cenotes make Akumal diving a singular experience and have won the area worldwide recognition.

Akumal has always attracted travelers looking for a quiet, out-of-the way spot to soak up the sun, not to mention the excellent diving and snorkeling offshore.

All of the major resorts along the coast rent snorkeling equipment and scuba diving equipment. If they do not have a dive operation on the premises, most likely they are affiliated with one nearby. The rates are similar to what you would expect throughout the Caribbean. Most of the dive operators have scuba instructors on staff who are qualified to teach resort courses and open water certifications.

Playacar Divers' fast boats are typical of dive boats used by Mexican dive operators.

◄ *Cannons recovered from sunken Spanish galleons line the bay in Akumal.*

5

Diving and Snorkeling in Cancun

In Cancun, visibility varies depending on whether you are diving on reefs inside or outside of the bay and between summer and winter seasons. There can be a lot of thermocline and this, too, affects the water clarity. Winter water conditions can also be choppier as there is generally more wind than during the calmer summer months.

In Cancun, four reefs including Chitales and El Bajito that lie in about 40 feet of water between Cancun and Isla Mujeres off Punta Cancun offer snorkelers and beginner divers a good opportunity to observe the variety and color of the marine environment in the area. There is also a shallow reef near the southern part and novice snorkelers will find almost no current there.

Generally, the further out you go into the open ocean, the better the visibility tends to be. Unfortunately, the reefs are a little deeper and there is almost always a current, which can sometimes be quite strong. If you are an experienced diver, however, you will want to try the reefs outside the bay

Dive Site Ratings

	Novice Diver	Novice Diver w/ Instructor or Divemaster	Intermediate Diver w/ Instructor or Divemaster	Intermediate Diver	Advanced Diver	Advanced Diver w/ Instructor or Divemaster
1 Caves of the Sleeping Sharks				x		
2 Los Manchones	x					
3 Los Cuevones*	x					
4 Cuevas de Afuera				x		
5 El Tunel					x	
6 Grampin Reef					x	
7 Keep Reef			x			

* Good snorkeling area

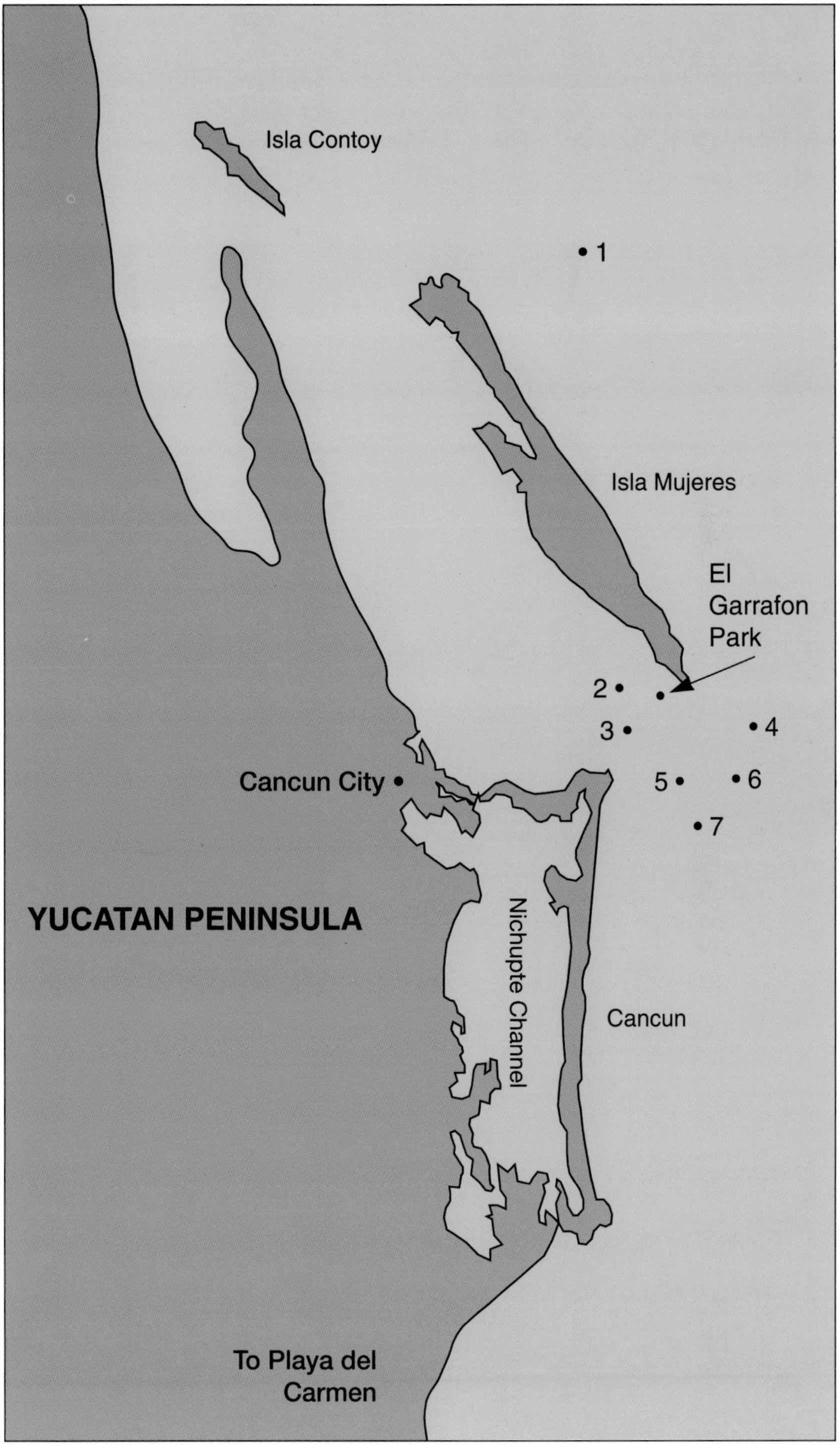

Isla Contoy

• 1

Isla Mujeres

El Garrafon Park

2 •

3 •

• 4

Cancun City •

5 •

• 6

• 7

YUCATAN PENINSULA

Nichupte Channel

Cancun

To Playa del Carmen

or seek out the challenge of exploring the *Ultrafreeze,* a wreck situated in 110 feet of water about 8 miles east of Isla Mujeres.

Most of the sites in and outside of the bay are visited by dive operators from Cancun and Isla Mujeres. Avid snorkelers should strongly consider a trip to El Garrafon Park off Isla Mujeres, a national marine park that is included in most day-excursions to Isla Mujeres from Cancun.

Angelfish make an appearance on every dive in the Cancun area.

Paamul—Xpuha—Kantenah—Yalku

As you cruise southward along the coastal highway, the road runs parallel to the sea surrounded by dense jungle. Continuing in a southerly direction from Playa del Carmen, you'll notice several dirt roads on the left side, some marked and others unmarked, that seem to lead into the jungle. If you follow them, you'll discover some of the most beautiful beaches in the Caribbean.

After a short ride you'll arrive at Paamul Beach. It is a small rocky beach surrounded by a picturesque coconut grove. The beach has campsites and cabins as well as a small restaurant and offers seclusion and privacy for those who want to escape the crowds. If you happen to be there during the summer turtle nesting season, you might see some turtles laying their eggs on the beach at night. Turtles are protected by the government all along this coast, so don't touch or harass them and don't shine any lights on them while they are in the process of digging their nests.

Heading southward again about 8 kilometers you'll find Xpuha, a beautiful white sand beach encircled by arching palm trees. When you find yourself in need of a break from the sun and sand, a short hike from the beach across the highway will take you to two privately owned cenotes, El Cenote and Cenote Azul. Filled with crystal clear water, they make excellent and refreshing swimming holes.

At the end of yet another dirt turnoff is Kantenah Beach. You can spend the day swimming and snorkeling here, but this is one of those places where you can be content just "hanging out" in one of the many hammocks that dot the beach. The beach also features a palapa-style restaurant and beachside showers.

One kilometer beyond Kantenah is a small lagoon called Yalku. The short road that leads to the lagoon is unmarked. Similar to Xel-ha (see page **51**), this lagoon is ideal for snorkeling, especially if you're the type of snorkeler who doesn't appreciate crowds. It is very secluded and it is unlikely that you'll find more than one or two (if any!) other people here at the same time. You might notice that the water is sometimes a little hazy. This occurs when fresh water mixes with the salt water in the lagoon. But it shouldn't affect your enjoyment of this beautiful jungle refuge.

While these are beautiful beaches, many more along the road are just waiting to be discovered. Keep an eye out as you're driving along because every few miles there is bound to be a secret beach, cenote, or lagoon ripe for exploration!

This divemaster shows off his new-found friend, a webbed burrfish.

Caves of the Sleeping Sharks 1

Typical depth range:	60 to 70 feet
Typical current conditions:	Strong
Expertise required:	Intermediate w/ instructor or divemaster
Access:	Boat

A local fisherman diving off of the northeast coast of Isla Mujeres in the unsheltered waters of the open Caribbean Sea discovered a strange phenomenon of sharks lying, unmoving 70 feet below the surface. Sharks, of course, are supposed to need constant motion to breathe.

In the cover story of the April 1975 issue of *National Geographic* magazine, oceanographer and cinematographer Ramon Bravo documented the caves and the sharks, bringing it to public attention. But it was Jacques Cousteau and Dr. Eugenie Clark who made the "sleeping sharks" famous. The phenomenon is caused by fresh-water bubbles that emerge from underwater springs and apparently have an anesthetizing effect on the resident sharks.

The terrain at the dive site is a series of ridges that are densely carpeted with marine growth. Within the ridges are oversized limestone caves in which a variety of sharks find an ideal place to rest. Divers exploring this site are most likely to see nurse sharks, but you may be lucky and see a bull shark, black-tip, or lemon shark. In addition to the sharks, barracuda and schooling fish can always be found cruising the reef.

At the Caves of the Sleeping Sharks, divers often have an opportunity to view sharks close-up.

A dive at the Caves affords experienced divers a unique and fascinating opportunity to observe sharks at close hand.

There is generally a strong current at this site, and, combined with the 70 foot depth, it is generally recommended for experienced divers.

Large schools of grunts and snapper frequent most of the reefs around Bahia de Mujeres.

Los Manchones 2

Typical depth range:	30 to 60 feet
Typical current conditions:	None to slight surge
Expertise required:	Resort or novice
Access:	Boat

Located near the southern tip of Isla Mujeres inside of the bay lies a one-kilometer-long coral reef that is considered to be one of the best dive sites in the Cancun area. Averaging 30–50 feet deep with a maximum depth of 60 feet, it is one of the main attractions for divers.

A French angelfish entertains a diver on the sponge encrusted reef at Los Manchones.

The shy queen angelfish is one of the most colorful inhabitants of the Los Manchones reef.

As you descend on this site, you will discover beautiful expanses of staghorn and brain corals. Scattered coral heads rise 5–10 feet from the sea bottom. On closer examination, you will find a variety of macro creatures, especially colorful Christmas tree worms and delicate feather dusters swaying in the slight surge. Angelfish can always be relied on to make an appearance at this site as well.

While the reefs of Los Manchones offer the bright oranges and reds of encrusting corals typical of the Caribbean, what is most striking about this site is the enormous schools of grunts, chub, yellowtail snapper, and goatfish that cruise among the coral overhangs and seem unperturbed by the presence of curious divers.

Xel-Ha

Between Akumal and Tulum is Xel-Ha, pronounced "shell-ha." It is an unusual national park that centers around a large, landlocked lagoon, which is a natural aquarium and sanctuary for tropical fish which find their way into the pool through tunnels in the bedrock that connect to the ocean. Fishing is strictly prohibited but visitors are welcome to snorkel among the fish in designated areas and also explore an underwater Mayan shrine.

You can rent snorkel gear at the park and there are changing facilities as well. For those who want to stay dry, the active marine life below the crystal clear water can be seen from the walkways and platforms surrounding the lagoon.

At one time, Xel-Ha was a Mayan merchant marine port and across the road from the lagoon, you can see some archaeological ruins dating from the post-Classic period of the Mayan civilization.

Xel-Ha attracts visitors from all over the Cancun-Tulum Corridor who come to swim and snorkel in the clear, tropical fish-filled waters of its famous lagoon.

Los Cuevones 3

Typical depth range: 30 feet
Typical current conditions: Some current
Expertise required: Novice
Access: Boat

Located almost in the middle of Bahia de Mujeres, conveniently equidistant from both Cancun and Isla Mujeres is a relatively shallow site that is popular with divers and snorkelers alike. At a depth of only 30 feet, the reef at Los Cuevones offers snorkelers a bird's eye view of what a typical Caribbean reef looks like. But for divers who can get a close up view, the reef is alive with activity.

Los Cuevones attracts huge schools of porkfish that tend to seek shelter under the many ledges.

The blue angelfish is rarer than the queen angel, but its unusual coloring is unmistakable.

Surprisingly, this shallow reef that entertains so many divers is almost overrun with schooling fish. And while the species may not be unusual, the effect of seeing so many fish in one place is quite impressive.

The queen angelfish that tour the reef are easily identifiable by their distinctive neon turquoise and yellow coloring. Extremely shy and skittish when divers are in the area, they are most often found swimming in and out of the nooks and crannies carved in the sides of the reef. Watch them for a while and you'll notice that they swim the same "course" repeatedly. They are not easy to photograph but patience will ultimately pay off!

On the reef at Los Cuevones, golden and spotted moray eels are in residence and you can expect to see a few heads poking out of the safety of their holes. Look closely as you cruise along the reef, and you may find some decorator crabs. These make excellent subjects for macro photography.

Every so often, take a moment to look around you, especially in the sandy areas surrounding the reef where southern stingrays often stop to rest.

This is an ideal site to visit for newly certified divers.

Cuevas de Afuera (Outside Caves) 4

Typical depth range:	45 to 50 feet
Typical current conditions:	Moderate
Expertise required:	Intermediate with instructor or divemaster
Access:	Boat

Outside of the Bahia de Mujeres (the bay that separates Cancun from Isla Mujeres), lie several of the best dives in the Cancun/Isla Mujeres area. Among the outer group of sites is a particularly pretty one called Cuevas de Afuera or Outside Caves. The reef lies at a depth of about 50 feet with the top of the ledge at about 45 feet. Although it is not a particularly deep dive, it is recommended for intermediate divers because at times the current can get a bit too strong for less experienced divers.

This Cancun divemaster explores the colorful reefs at Cuevas de Afuera.

Visibility on the site averages about 50–60 feet and there is plenty to see.

Ledges formed by the reef as well as a number of scattered coral islands attract populous schools of fish. Schooling porkfish, in particular, are in abundance, seeking shelter beneath the many overhangs. You'll also find barracuda "hanging out" and watching the activity on the reef with their customary curiosity.

The French angelfish, by the way, are huge!

Cuevas de Afuera is a virtual playground for divers. Cruising along the reef, you'll discover archways, a number of long, low swimthroughs and a few caves that are big enough to explore. Occasionally, nurse sharks can be found in these protected areas. There is even a tunnel that extends about 15 feet through the reef and is large enough for divers to swim through. Those swimming above on the reef can follow your progress by the bubbles that escape through the porous coral composition.

Although the top of the reef is decorated by delicate lavender sea fans, it is also adorned by stinging hydroids and fire coral, so exercise a little caution when peering closely in search of spotted morays that might be in the nooks and crannies. No matter how fascinating the reef activity might be, look around you so you don't miss the spotted eagle ray that might pass a few feet above you!

Expect to encounter at least moderate current on this site. The current tends to be stronger at the surface and usually slackens once you reach the reef. The descent line dropped by your divemaster will provide any assistance you might need submerging in the right place and, once on the bottom, the reef's ledges offer protection against whatever current you might encounter there.

Cuevas de Afuera's many tunnels and overhangs make ideal habitats for large schools of grunts and snappers.

El Tunel (The Tunnel) 5

Typical Depth Range:	55 feet
Typical current conditions:	Strong up to 2 knots
Expertise required:	Advanced
Access:	Boat

El Tunel is another of Cancun's "numero uno" dives. Like Grampin and Outside Caves, it is situated outside of the bay and washed by the nourishing currents of the open Caribbean Sea. Its name is appropriately derived from its main feature—a large tunnel that extends through the reef for about 15 feet and can accommodate two to three divers swimming through at the same time.

A diver is astounded by the brilliant colors blanketing the overhangs at El Tunel.

A diver peers through a hole in the reef at El Tunel decorated by orange elephant ear sponges and red encrusting sponges.

Generally, the reef has a 5–6-foot-high profile similar to other reefs in the vicinity. The marine life is prolific and the reef displays an abundance of aquatic vegetation. Ledges, overhangs, nooks, and crannies provide an intricate habitat for a wide variety of sea creatures, and you will almost always find at least one sleeping nurse shark here and perhaps several.

Its location beyond the bay also brings in some of the creatures that are more readily found in open ocean. It is possible to encounter sea turtles and even dolphins.

The dive is rated for advanced divers with experience because, although the maximum depth is only around 55 feet, divers are likely to encounter very strong currents that new divers will have difficulty handling. Nevertheless, it is one of Cancun's premiere dives.

Grampin Reef 6

Typical depth range:	55 feet
Typical current conditions:	Generally strong up to 2 knots
Expertise required:	Advanced
Access:	Boat

If you were to take a consensus among local divemasters in Cancun, most likely each of them would name Grampin Reef as one of the very best dives.

This dive site is one of the farthest from the bay, sitting at the edge of the open ocean. The reef extends for about a mile. There is no mooring system on these dive sites to protect them from being fished out by local fishermen, but the divemasters and captains are experienced and knowledgeable and have no difficulty putting divers on the best sites.

The Grampin Reef dive site is characterized by ledges that rise 6–7 feet from the seabed as well as scattered coral heads. Some of these ledges form caves that go through the reef and are quite colorful.

As you'll discover is typical of the sites inside and outside of the bay, there is no shortage of schooling fish inhabiting anyplace where there is an overhang or ledge. Hordes of blue-striped grunts, porkfish, and yellowtail snappers hover almost motionlessly, moving only as far as is necessary to avoid intruding divers. You can also count on finding a few pairs of angelfish cruising slowly enough to photograph or videotape.

On the outside or ocean side of the reef, there is always the possibility of spotting sharks, eagle rays, dolphin and even an occasional turtle.

Purple sea fans and encrusting sponges create a colorful underwater tapestry at Grampin Reef.

Keep Reef 7

Typical depth range:	45 to 60 feet
Typical current conditions:	Medium to strong on surface
Expertise required:	Intermediate
Access:	Boat

Although it doesn't appear on the dive site maps in the tourist magazines you'll find in Cancun, Keep Reef is one of the better dives in the area. Lying at about 45 feet at the top of the reef and 60 feet at the base, Keep Reef is a ledge-like formation shaped like a horseshoe and riddled with swimthroughs, arches, and numerous overhangs that are heavily shrouded in vibrant orange and red encrusting sponges. Because these colors are less vivid to the eye in natural light, bring a dive light with you. The artificial light, even during the day, will reveal the true intensity of the colors. However, you won't need the aid of a light to enjoy the beautiful purple sea fans and orange elephant ear sponges that decorate the reef.

This dive site is loaded with schooling fish. Large populations of French and blue-striped grunts, porkfish, and Bermuda chub crowd around the coral ledges and overhangs seemingly undaunted by the presence of divers. They may move slightly when a diver approaches, but don't expect them to vacate their place on the reef for you and your dive buddy! Golden and white-spotted morays seek shelter in the reef's pockets and occasionally emerge to find another protective hole. French and gray angelfish cruise along the reef and you may see a scrawled filefish looking for food. Small nurse shark may be lurking under archways or, more likely, just taking a nap.

On this dive, it's worth taking your eyes off the reef action occasionally to look around you. You're likely to see a good size school of barracuda or even a few eagle rays nonchalantly passing by.

Visibility is generally 60–70 feet although it varies with the season and water conditions.

At the surface, the current, which runs perpendicular to reef, can be quite strong. To make the ascent to the reef easy for divers, the divemaster usually drops a descent line from the boat. Once on the reef, the current is usually substantially reduced. If you swim near the bottom, the reef offers additional protection from the current.

There is quite a bit of fire coral on top of reef, so be careful to avoid brushing up against it or grabbing it. It may look like dead coral, but it packs an uncomfortable sting.

6

Playa del Carmen

Although Playa del Carmen is essentially a small coastal fishing village, the resort development over the last few years has increased its attraction to divers. The largest resort, Continental Plaza Playacar, which lies on a pristine beach, has a full-service dive operation on the premises, and Las Palapas, a more intimate resort located just outside town, also has a dive operation. Both are equipped to take divers to the best reefs in the area.

If you plan to dive in Playa del Carmen, don't expect everything to operate like clockwork. Dive boats don't necessarily depart exactly when they schedule the dive trip and you may spend more time waiting than you are accustomed to in other dive destinations or at home. But remember . . . you're in Mexico and everyone is very, very laidback. So relax and soak up the sun!

Dive Site Ratings

	Novice Diver	Novice Diver w/ Instructor or Divemaster	Intermediate Diver w/ Instructor or Divemaster	Intermediate Diver	Advanced Diver	Advanced Diver w/ Instructor or Divemaster
8 The Arch					x	
9 Coral Heads	x					
10 The Balconies					x	
11 The Tarpons		x				
12 Barracuda Reef		x				

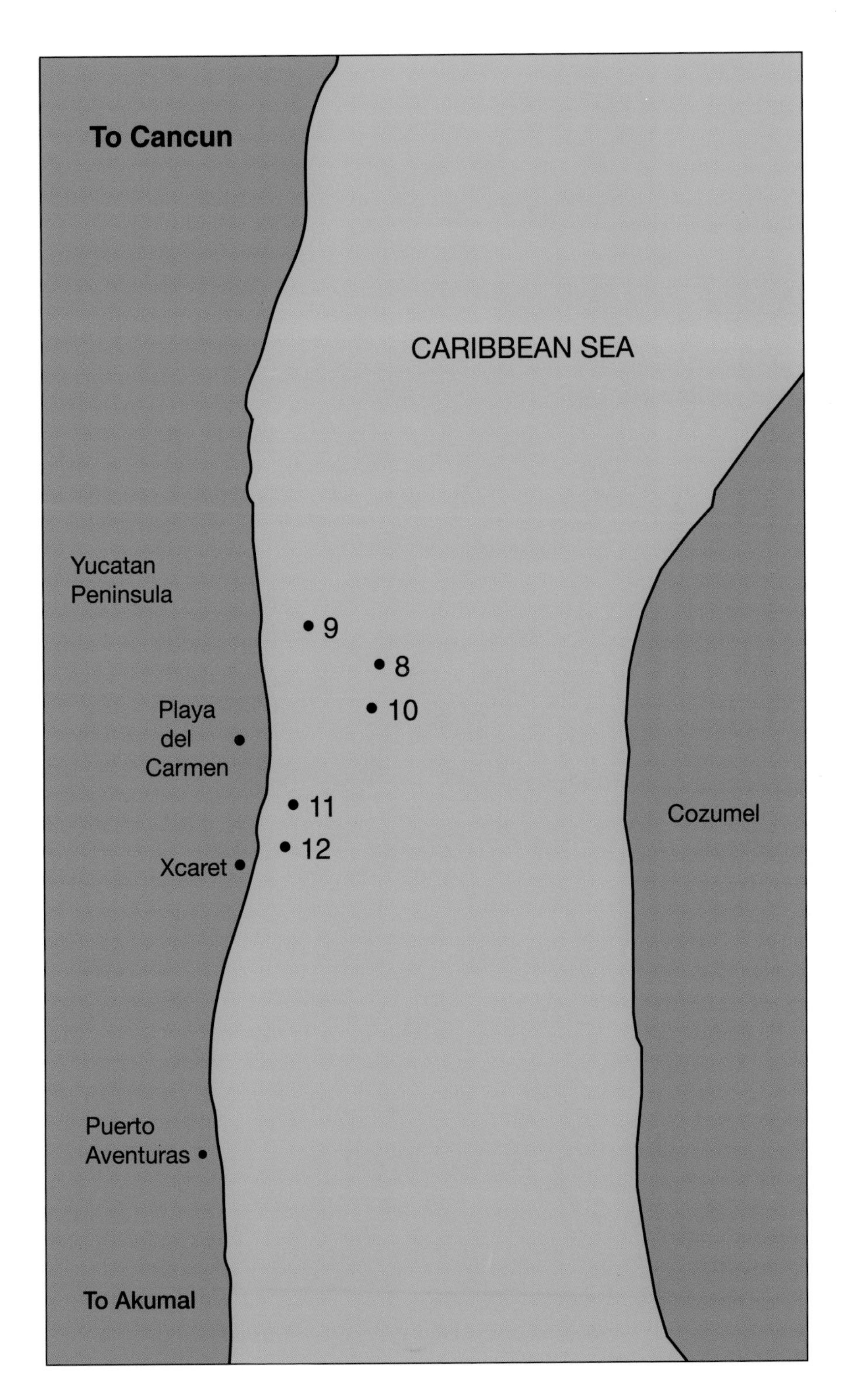
To Cancun
CARIBBEAN SEA
Yucatan
Peninsula
9
8
10
Playa
del
Carmen
11
12
Xcaret
Cozumel
Puerto
Aventuras
To Akumal

You are likely to find a starfish in the sandy areas between the shallow reefs in the Playa del Carmen area.

The Arch 8

Typical depth range: 80 to 100 feet
Typical current conditions: None to strong
Expertise required: Intermediate to Advanced
Access: Boat

Located approximately 6 miles north of Playa del Carmen, the Arch is one of the popular drift dives in the Playa del Carmen area. The reef at this site runs parallel to the shore and varies in depth from 80 to 100 feet. Depending on the strength of the current, which runs south to north, divemasters will usually begin the dive about an ⅛ mile or more from the Arch and enable divers to drift toward the Arch to finish the dive.

The coral growth along the reef leading to the Arch is lush and colorful.

An arrowcrab finds shelter among the protective tentacles of a sea anemone not far from the Arch.

Buffeted on both sides by immense "rivers" of white sand, the reef itself features lots of overhangs and ledges that provide a playground for a wide variety of Caribbean marine life. Coral growth is mainly concentrated on the top of the reef, but divers will see brightly colored encrusting sponges, bent and twisted barrel sponges, and orange elephant ear sponges in addition to the usual soft corals typical of the area.

As divers near the end of the drift dive, the Arch comes into view. It is a worthy climax to the dive, standing 20 feet tall and having a 30-foot span. It clearly dominates the reefscape and, although the coral growth on the Arch may not be as prolific or dense as it is on other parts of the reef, there is always a large school of jacks swimming in and out of the Arch, creating a dramatic and memorable effect before divers ascend to the boat.

Coral Heads 9

Typical depth range: 15 to 35 feet
Typical current conditions: None to moderate
Expertise required: Novice
Access: Boat

The Playa del Carmen area has some excellent shallow dive sites ideal for beginner divers, as well as more seasoned divers, and Coral Heads is one of them. Between 15 and 35 feet of water, you'll discover 7 or 8 huge coral heads that stand as high as 10 to 15 feet above the seafloor. The coral heads are primarily composed of brain coral, sheet coral, ribbon, or lettuce corals. But interspersed with the hard coral growth are orange encrusting sponges and small barrel sponges that fill the gaps in between the huge coral formations.

Graceful stands of delicate pillar coral and brain coral, as well as elkhorn coral, can also be found at this site. During the day, divers can expect to see a lot of queen angelfish, parrotfish, sergeant majors, hogfish, large grouper, and amberjacks. But this is also a popular habitat for Caribbean spider crabs, lobster, and octopus which seem to be attracted to the ample hiding places created by the coral growth. These marine residents emerge at night to scavenge along the reef for food and also make this an excellent night dive site.

At Coral Heads, the reef is punctuated by many coral formations, but none is as dramatic as the pillar coral.

The Balconies 10

Typical depth range:	90 to 130 feet
Typical current conditions:	Medium to strong
Expertise required:	Advanced
Access:	Boat

Just north of Playa del Carmen is a wall dive called the Balconies, appropriately named for the stair-stepped manner in which the reef descends to the depths. The formation creates an effect of a series of balconies on a building.

The strong current at Balconies tends to twist and distort the large barrel sponges on the reef.

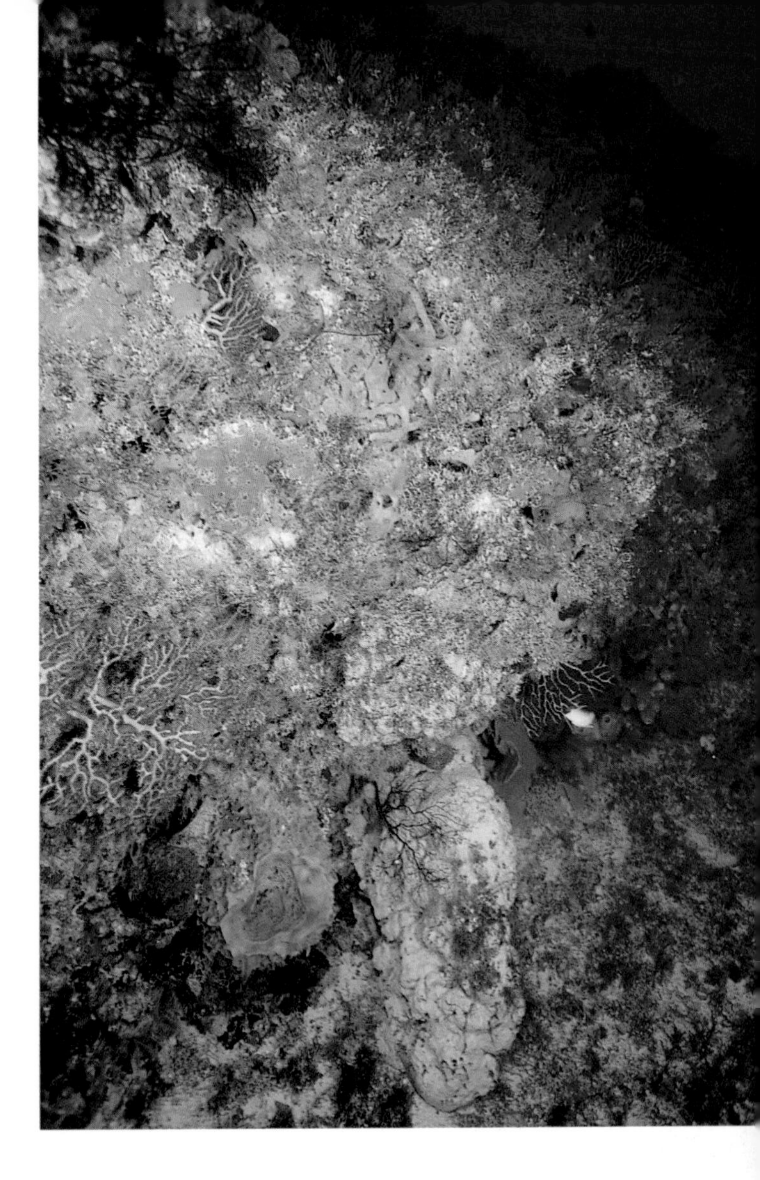

The stair-stepping deep reef at Balconies is home to a wide variety of brightly colored corals and sponges.

It is a deep dive, with the wall beginning at about 90 feet, so it is recommended for advanced divers who have previously logged dives at similar depths.

There is an excellent chance of encountering large turtles and nurse sharks on the Balconies. Look for them resting or sleeping on the edge of the wall. If you keep your head turning and looking up and down, you might even spot a large Atlantic manta ray, tiger grouper, or even a shark.

One of the striking aspects of this dive site is the collection of bent and contorted barrel sponges that seem to appear over the entire area of the dive site. Their unusual twisted appearance is a result of the ever-present current that runs south to north at this site.

Cenotes

You don't have to be an expert cave diver to see spectacular stalactites and stalagmites. You can take a snorkel or dive in a "cenote." Cenotes, or sinkholes, are produced when the roof of an underground cave collapses. The result is the formation of a deep water-filled well or hole that is accessible from the surface. These cenotes generally lead into a series of interconnected underground caves decorated with stalactites, stalagmites, and unusual formations. The water is crystal clear and the view can be spectacular. There are several cenotes along the Cancun-Tulum Corridor that are open to the public and where you can hire the services of a qualified cenote guide.

A cenote, a sinkhole formed when the ceiling of an underground cave collapses, offers visitors an unusual "swimming hole" in a jungle setting.

The Tarpons 11

Typical depth range: 30 to 50 feet
Typical current conditions: Moderate
Expertise required: Novice with instructor or divemaster
Access: Boat

If you were to continue to swim along the Barracuda Reef approximately a half mile north of the dive site that bears its name, you would come upon another site called the Tarpons. It is essentially a continuation of the same reef, perhaps not quite as prolific as the more southern section of the reef, but there is plenty to see, especially if you like big fish.

The Tarpons is a good place to see great amberjacks that cruise along the reefs.

The reef here exhibits a lot of ledge-like formations, which turn into tunnels permeating the reef. It is an ideal habitat for marine life. Most likely you'll be greeted at the Tarpons by large schools of tarpon and amberjacks that measure as much as 2½–3½ feet in length. They are not overly skittish and you can approach them fairly easily as long as you move in slowly. If you're particularly lucky and alert, you might see a small black tipped shark that makes an occasional appearance to chase the tarpon.

Cubera, pompanos, and 30–60-pound snapper also frequent this site. According to the local divemasters, these hefty marine critters can always be found here where a substantial amount of fresh water enters the sea near this section of the reef.

It is not unusual to see shimmering tarpon at the dive site named after them.

Barracuda Reef 12

Typical depth range:	25 to 50 feet
Typical current conditions:	None to strong
Expertise required:	Novice with instructor or divemaster
Access:	Boat

Just north of Xcaret Channel lies Barracuda Reef, a shallow dive site that offers divers of all levels an opportunity to explore the formations and active marine life typical of the Caribbean. Here the reef runs parallel to the

Not far from Xcaret, Barracuda Reef is a popular place for beginners and resort course divers.

The mini-wall and many overhangs that dominate Barracuda Reef make it a relaxing and interesting dive for experienced divers.

shoreline and begins as shallow as 25 feet. Along this top reef, a scattering of soft corals, especially sea whips, sea plumes, and stinging hydroids sway gracefully in the slight current.

The reef then drops to 35–50 feet forming a steep slope in areas. Along the steeper part of the reef, divers will also find a mini-wall featuring some small caves, as well as some sizable overhangs that extend out as much as 20 feet. Along the face of the sloping part of the reef, encrusting sponges predominantly in brilliant hues of orange and red intermix with gray tube sponges, small gorgonians, and azure vase sponges. The overall effect makes this a very colorful dive.

Green moray eels and spotted morays hide in the nooks and crannies that pock the reef. If you swim slowly about two feet off the reef, you are likely to find at least one poking its head out of its habitat. Several pairs of large gray and French angelfish also play along this reef. Because they tend to be fairly unfazed by divers, they make excellent subjects for underwater photography and video. Although not as easy to photograph but exquisite in their exotic coloration, queen angelfish and blue angelfish occasionally make an appearance along the reef as well. As you cruise along the edge of the reef, keep an eye out for large groups of conies.

Although occasionally strong winds can churn up the sand that runs parallel to the reef, visibility is usually very good on Barracuda Reef.

There is almost always some current on this dive site, but because of the shallow depth, it should not present a problem for even the most inexperienced certified diver.

Xcaret

Not far from Playa del Carmen is Xcaret, an important Mayan ceremonial center and seaport for over ten centuries. Today, it is a privately owned park that features, among other things, a series of underwater tunnels and cenotes as well as lagoons, natural pools, a natural inlet, and a beautiful beach. Visitors can take a forty-five minute underground excursion floating along the sub-surface river, spend the day snorkeling or diving among the tropical fish, visit with the resident dolphins, go horseback riding, or explore the Mayan ruins that have only recently been excavated. There is charge for admission to the park and daily bus service is available from Cancun.

7

Smart, Safe Diving

Preparation

Before you leave home, make sure all of your dive gear is in good working order and that all items that must be serviced yearly—especially regulators—have been. There is nothing as aggravating as getting on the boat, arriving on your first dive site, only to discover that your octopus is free-flowing. If you wear a mask with a prescription or have trouble finding a mask that fits you correctly, bring a backup mask. Masks have been known to arrive at a different destination than you, fall overboard, or break. You won't be comfortable with a borrowed mask if you can't see or if it keeps leaking. Finally, if you haven't been diving for 6 months or more, especially if you have logged fewer than 20 dives, it might be a good idea to take a practice or refresher dive either in a local pool at home or with an instructor at one of the resorts before you head for deep water.

Reef Etiquette and Buoyancy Control

Some dive sites along the Mexican Caribbean have moorings, but most do not. But regardless of whether sites are protected against anchor damage, there is nothing to protect them from damage by divers . . . except divers. Dive sites tend to be located where the reefs and walls display the most beautiful corals and sponges. And it only takes a moment—an inadvertently placed hand or knee on the coral or an unaware brush or kick with a fin—to destroy this fragile living part of our delicate ecosystem, to make a dive site a little less spectacular for other divers. Luckily, it only takes a little extra preparation and consideration to preserve it for generations of divers to come.

So if you're a new diver, a little rusty after a long hiatus on dry land, diving with new equipment, or if you just haven't paid much attention to your reef etiquette or buoyancy control in the past, here are a few helpful tips how you can personally help preserve our underwater environment:

A diver demonstrates proper buoyancy control hovering near a sponge encrusted overhang. ▶

Environmentally Aware

The unspoiled beauty of the Mexican Caribbean is not an accident. From the impressive Biosphere Reserve of Sian Ka'an in the southern region of Quintana Roo to the waters of Cancun, Isla Mujeres, and Cozumel, the Mexican government has instituted a comprehensive program of environmentally protected destinations. Included among these target sites are Punta Laguna, where the habitats of spider monkeys and exotic birds are protected, and Rio Lagaros, which boasts the largest flock of pink flamingos in North America.

On the reefs between Cancun and Isla Mujeres, divers are prohibited from touching or taking any of the fragile coral, creatures, or shells. In fact, the entire Mexican Caribbean is a protected national marine park. There are more than 500 species of tropical fish on the coral reefs in these waters and spearfishing is illegal. As divemasters will remind you, "take only pictures and leave only bubbles." And on Isla Contoy, tread gently because everything is protected!

Weight Yourself Properly. Never dive with too much weight. (northern divers—this means you! When you put on a lighter wetsuit or dive skin, shed some of those lead pounds, too!) Weight yourself so that you *float at eye level* on the surface with your lungs full of air and none in your BCD. Exhale fully and you should begin to sink. As your week of diving goes by and you relax underwater, drop some more weight. Ask your divemaster what kind of tank you're using. Tanks vary in their buoyancy when they are empty. You want to be able to hover comfortably at 15 feet to make your safety stop when your tank is low at the end of your dive.

Control Your Buoyancy with Your Breathing. If you are properly weighted and have successfully attained neutral buoyancy with your BCD at depth, you should be able to fine-tune your hovering capacity by inhaling and exhaling. Being able to rise and sink at will is the real trick to being able to hover, float and glide over and around the reef formations with grace and skill.

Avoid Fin Damage to Coral. Never stand (or kneel) on the corals. If you're hovering above the reef, keep your fins up off the reef. If you're swimming, do so in a horizontal position looking down so you're not flutter-kicking the reef. When you're cruising through a narrow space such as a tunnel or gully

◀ *Using only one finger, a diver is able to steady herself without grabbing, kicking, or standing on the reef.*

between coral heads, keep an eye on where your feet are and, if necessary, make your kicks small and efficient to move you through the compact area. Reef etiquette also demands that, if you are swimming near a sandy bottom, stay several feet above the sand so you don't kick up any silt and ruin the dive for other divers or smother the delicate corals and sponges with sand.

Don't Touch the Reef. No matter how pretty and tactile the coral and sponges are, look but don't touch. Never, never grab onto the reef to steady yourself. If you need to stabilize yourself or keep from bumping into things or other divers, try using one or two fingers instead of your entire hand. And look for dead spots, areas between the corals or even the underside of a coral cranny where there is generally less growth. If, by chance, you see any trash on the reef, bring it up with you. If we all do our part, it will make a difference.

Watch Where You Land. If you need to touch down or kneel on solid ground, look for a sandy area in between the coral heads. If you need to take a photo, float or glide over your subject or steady yourself with a finger, but keep the rest of your body away from the reef. If you can't get the picture or see your subject without lying on the coral . . . don't take the picture!

The fierce looking moray eel is harmless unless provoked or surprised by an intruding diver.

Don't Drag Loose Gauges or Octopus Across the Reef. Hanging consoles, goody bags, tools, and other unsecured equipment can do as much damage to the corals as your hands and feet. Keep your equipment close to your body by tucking them into your BCD pockets or using retainer clips.

Don't Grab the Marine Creatures. Don't ride the turtles, grab the lobsters, chase the stingrays, or harass the eels. They are curious by nature and will gradually move toward you or stay still if you leave them alone. If you grab them, they'll disappear faster than you can clear your mask . . . and no one else will have a chance to see them either.

Be considerate. Leave the reef in the same condition in which you find it. In this way, it will remain healthy and thriving for future divers to enjoy.

Hazardous Marine Life

Diving along the Mexican Caribbean isn't really hazardous. It's divers who are hazardous. When was the last time a stand of fire coral pursued a diver to sting him? Most stings, scrapes, and punctures are due to divers inadvertently bumping into coral or touching a creature that instinctively defends itself against its giant aggressor. Some are harmless and merely uncomfortable. Others may require medical attention. Ideally, we shouldn't be touching anything underwater, but it does happen and it does hurt!

Fire Coral. Mustard brown in color, fire coral is most often found in shallower waters encrusting dead gorgonians or coral. Contact causes a burning sensation that lasts for several minutes and sometimes causes red welts on the skin. If you rub against fire coral, do not try to rub the affected area as you will spread the small stinging particles. Upon resurfacing, apply meat tenderizer to relieve the sting and then antibiotic cream. Cortisone cream can also reduce any inflammation.

Stinging Hydroids. These creatures generally disguise themselves as delicately lacy black or white plumes that grow between one inch and one foot tall. While they attract the eye with their pretty appearance, you won't find them so pleasant to the touch. Initially they feel like a pin prick, but the sting can last for a while and can cause welts. Treat it as you would fire coral stings . . . and don't be fooled the next time!

Sponges. They may be beautiful but sponges can also pack a powerful punch with fine spicules that sting on contact. While bright reddish brown ones are often the stinging kind, familiarly called "dread red," they are not the only culprits. If you touch a stinging sponge, scrape the area with the edge of your dive knife. Home remedies include mild vinegar or ammonia

solutions to ease the pain, but most of it should subside within a day. Again, cortisone cream might help.

Sea Urchins. The urchin's most dangerous weapon is its spines, which can penetrate neoprene wetsuits, booties, and gloves with ease. You'll know you've been jabbed from the instant pain. Urchins tend to be more common in shallow areas near shore and come out of their shelters under coral heads at night. If you are beach diving, beware of urchins that may be lying on the shallow reef you have to cross to reach deeper water. Don't move across it on your hands and knees, and start swimming as soon as possible. Injuries should be attended to as soon as possible because infection can occur. Minor punctures require removal of the spine and treatment with an antibiotic cream. More serious ones should be looked at by a doctor.

Bristle Worms. Bristle worms make a great subject for macro photography but don't touch them to move them to the perfect spot. Use a strobe arm or dive knife. Contact will result in tiny stinging bristles being embedded in the skin and a burning feeling or welt. You can try to scrape the bristles off with the edge of a dive knife. Otherwise, they will work themselves out within a few days. Again, cortisone cream can help minimize any inflammation. Do not rub the infected area.

Sea Wasps. A potentially serious diving hazard, sea wasps are small, potent jellyfish with four stinging tentacles and they generally swim within a few feet of the surface at night. If sea wasps have been spotted in the water where you are planning to do a night dive, take caution. Don't linger on the surface upon entry into the water. When you return, turn your dive light off as it attracts them and exit the water as quickly as possible. Their sting is very painful and leaves a red welt as a reminder. Do NOT try to push them away from your area of ascent by sending air bubbles to the surface from your regulator. The bubbles may break off their tentacles and you won't be able to see where the stinging tentacles are. If you are allergic to bee stings and sea wasps have been spotted at the dive site, consider foregoing the dive as you will most likely have the same reaction to a sea wasp sting.

Stonefish. They may be one of the sea's best camouflaged creatures, but if you receive a puncture by the poisonous spines that are hidden among its fins, you'll know you've found a stonefish. They tend to lie on the bottom on coral, so, unless you are lying on the bottom or on the reef—which you shouldn't be (see "Reef Etiquette and Buoyancy Control"), they shouldn't present a problem. Should you get stung, go to a hospital or a doctor as soon

◀ ***The strong currents in the Mexican Caribbean encourage the growth of stinging hydroids, which can vary in color from white to black.***

The camouflaging colors of the stonefish can make it difficult to see this venomous fish hiding against the coral.

as possible, because it can result in severe allergic reactions, much pain, and infection.

Stingrays. These creatures are harmless, unless you sit or step on them. If you harass them, you may discover the long, barbed stinger located at the base of the tail. This stinger wields a very painful wound that can be deep and become infected. If you suffer from a sting, go to a hospital or seek a doctor's care immediately. But the best policy is to leave them alone, and they'll leave you alone in return.

Eels. Similarly, eels won't bother you unless you bother them. It is best not to hand feed them, especially when you don't know if other eels or hazardous fish such as barracuda or sharks are in the area. And don't put your hand in a dark hole. It might just house an eel. Eels have extremely poor eyesight and cannot always distinguish between food and your hand. If you are bitten by an eel, don't try to pull your hand away—their teeth are extraordinarily sharp. Let the eel release it, and then surface (at the required slow rate of ascent), apply first aid, and then head for the nearest hospital.

Sharks. Although not an extremely common sight for divers, when sharks do appear, it is a cause for celebration and fascination. As a rule, most of the sharks you will encounter along Mexico's Caribbean coast are not aggressive and will not attack divers. However, do not feed them or harass them. If you are unlucky enough to be mistaken for a meal, the nearest hospital is the most logical next stop.

Barracuda. Barracudas have a miserable reputation. In fact, they are somewhat shy although unnervingly curious. They will hover near enough to divers to observe what they are so interested in, but just try to photograph them and they keep their distance. You'll see them on most dives. Don't bother them, and they won't bother you.

Man o' Wars. These large purplish jellyfish have an air sac that suspends hundreds of very powerful stinging tentacles from it. Watch for them while ascending, swimming, or resting on the surface. You will see them more often during the winter months. If you are stung, see a doctor for treatment.

Sea Lice. Not much is known about these larval jellyfish that are invisible to the human eye except that they can cause itching and red splotchiness for several days after contact. They seem to be most prominent during the summer, when the water is warmer. To avoid sea lice, rinse your wetsuits and dive skins in fresh water when you come up from your dive and take a fresh water shower. If possible, change to a dry bathing suit after you finish diving. If you do suffer from sea lice, cortisone creme can help relieve some of the discomfort.

Diving Accidents

Diving is a safe sport and there are very few accidents compared to the number of divers and dives made each year. However, occasionally accidents do occur and emergency medical treatment should be sought immediately. If you are diving with a local dive operation, they will be equipped to handle any situation expediently. If a diving injury or decompression sickness occurs when you are on your own, here are some important emergency numbers to contact:

Cancun hospital	41818
Cancun police	41913
Divers Alert Network	(919) 684-8111
***Air Ambulance America of Mexico:**	95-800-222-3564
	512-479-8000

*24-hour standby to fly out sick or injured from any point in Mexico. You can get this service included with your DAN insurance.

Divers Alert Network/DAN

The Divers Alert Network (DAN), a non-profit membership association of individuals and organizations sharing a common interest in diving safety, assists in the treatment of underwater diving accidents by operating a 24-hour national telephone emergency hotline, (919) 684-8111 (collect calls are accepted), and to increase diver safety awareness through education.

DAN does not maintain any treatment facility nor does it directly provide any form of treatment, but is a service that complements existing medical systems. DAN's most important function is facilitating the entry of the injured diver into the hyperbaric trauma care system by coordinating the efforts of everyone involved in the victim's care.

Calls for routine information that do not concern a suspected diving injury or emergency should be directed to DAN information number (919) 684-2948 from 9 a.m. to 5 p.m. Monday–Friday Eastern Standard time. This number should not be called for general information or chamber locations. Chamber availability changes periodically making obsolete information dangerous at the time of an emergency. Instead, divers should contact DAN as soon as a diving emergency is suspected.

Hyperbaric treatment and air ambulance service can be costly. All divers who have comprehensive medical insurance should check to make sure that hyperbaric treatment and air ambulance services are adequately covered internationally. DAN membership includes insurance coverage specifically for dive injuries. Four different membership levels offering four different levels of coverage are available.

Membership ranges from $25–45 a year, which includes dive accident insurance, the DAN *Underwater Diving Accident Manual,* which summarizes each type of major diving injury and outlines procedures for initial management and care of the victim; a membership care listing diving related symptoms and DAN's emergency and non-emergency phone numbers; decals with DAN's logo and emergency number; and *Alert Diver,* a newsletter that provides information on diving medicine and safety in layman's language. Special memberships for dive stores, dive clubs, and corporations are available. The DAN Manual as well as membership information and applications can be obtained from the Administrative Coordinator, National Diving Alert Network, Duke University Medical Center, Box 3823, Durham, NC 27710.

When the infrequent injury does occur, DAN is prepared to help. DAN support currently comes from diver membership and contributions from the diving industry. It is a legal, non-profit public service organization and all donations are tax deductible.

Appendix 1: Dive and Watersports Operations

This list is included as a service to the reader. The authors and publisher have made every effort to make this list accurate at the time the book was printed. This list does not constitute an endorsement of these operators and dive shops. If operators/owners wish to be included in future reprints/editions, please contact Pisces Books, P.O. Box 2608, Houston, Texas 77252-2608.

Cancun

Aqua Tours
Paseo Kukulcan Km 6 1/4
PO Box 528
Cancun, Quintana Roo 77500
988-3-04-00, 3-11-37, 3-02-27
988-3-04-03 (fax)

Marina Aqua Ray
Blvd. Kukulcan Km 10.5
Hotel Zone, Cancun, Quintana Roo 77500
988-3-30-07, 3-17-63, 3-11-73

Marina Mundo Water World
P.O. Box 166
Cancun, Quintana Roo 77500
988-3-05-54

Nautilus Diving
Marina del Hotel Caribbean Suites
Galeon D9 Hotel Zone
Cancun, Quintana Roo
988-4-49-67 (ph/fax)

Royal Yacht Club
Blvd. Kukulcan at Royal Mayan and Omni Hotels
Cancun, Quintana Roo
988-5-32-60 (ph/fax)

Scuba Cancun
Blvd. Kukulcan Km 5
Hotel Zone, Cancun, Quintana Roo
988-3-10-11, 4-23-36

Solo Buceo
Hotel Camino Real
P.O. Box 621
Cancun, Quintana Roo
988-3-01-00, 3-12-00, 4-20-66 ext 8715

Isla Mujeres

Carnavalito Dive Shop
Av. R. Medina #7
Esq. Madero
Isla Mujeres, Quintana Roo
987-7-01-18 (ph/fax)

Delfin Diving
P.O. Box 25
Isla Mujeres, Quintana Roo 77400
988-2-02-74
703-836-2518 (U.S.)

Mexico Divers
P.O. Box 87
Isla Mujeres, Quintana Roo 77400
988-2-02-74

Playa del Carmen

Buceo Cyan-Ha
Hotel Shangri-la Caribe
APDO, Postal 116
Playa del Carmen, Quintana Roo 77710
987-2-28-88 (ph/fax)

Mike Madden's Cedam Dive Centers
Puerto Aventuras-Aventuras Akumal
P.O. Box 117
Playa del Carmen, Quintana Roo 77710
987-2-22-33
987-4-13-39 (ph/fax)

Playacar Divers
Continental Plaza Playacar
Fracc. Playacar
Playa del Carmen, Quintana Roo 77710
987-3-01-00 (hotel)
987-3-01-05 (hotel fax)

Akumal

The Akumal Dive Shop
Postal #1
Playa del Carmen, Quintana Roo 77710
987-4-12-59
988-4-00-06 (fax)

Appendix 2: Further Reading

Alevizon, W. S., *Caribbean Reef Ecology,* Pisces Books, Houston, TX, 1993.

Barnes, Robert D., *Invertebrate Zoology,* Saunders College/Holt, Rinehart and Winston, Philadelphia, PA, 1980.

Colin, P., *Caribbean Reef Invertebrates and Plants,* T.F.H. Publishing Co., Neptune City, NJ, 1987.

Cotter, Daniel T., Thomas P. Thompson, and Ephey B. Priest, *Wrecks of Broward,* Dive Vision, Margate, FL, 1991.

Greenberg, I. and J., *Waterproof Guide to Corals and Fishes,* Seahawk Press, Miami, FL, 1977.

Humann, Paul, *Reef Creature Identification,* New World Publications, Jacksonville, FL, 1992.

Humann, Paul, *Reef Fish Identification,* New World Publications, Jacksonville, FL, 1989.

Humfrey, Michael, *Sea Shells of the West Indies,* Collins, London, England, 1975.

Kaplan, Eugene H., *A Field Guide to Coral Reefs,* Houghton Mifflin Company, Boston, MA, 1982.

Meinkoth, Norman A., *The Audubon Society Field Guide to North American Seashore Creatures,* Knopf, New York, NY, 1981.

Pisces Photo Pak of Caribbean Reef Fish, Pisces Books, Houston, TX, 1990.

Wilson R. and J., *Watching Fishes: A Guide to Coral Reef Fish Behavior,* Pisces Books, Houston, TX, 1985/1992.

Index

Like these marvelous Christmastree worms, Cancun and the secluded villages to the south offer an exquisite mélange of simplicity and extravagance.